50 Premium Noodle Recipes

By: Kelly Johnson

Table of Contents

- Truffle Mac and Cheese
- Lobster Fettuccine Alfredo
- Thai Pad Thai
- Beef Stroganoff with Egg Noodles
- Carbonara with Pancetta
- Miso Ramen with Soft-Boiled Egg
- Lobster Bisque Noodles
- Shrimp Scampi with Linguine
- Butternut Squash Ravioli
- Peking Duck Noodles
- Szechuan Noodles
- Sweet Potato Gnocchi
- Braised Pork Belly Ramen
- Garlic Butter Shrimp Pasta
- Tofu and Veggie Stir-Fry Noodles
- Zucchini Noodles with Pesto
- Braised Short Rib Pasta

- Green Curry Noodles
- Truffle Macaroni
- Pad See Ew
- Korean Japchae (Stir-Fried Glass Noodles)
- Beef and Broccoli Udon
- Spicy Szechuan Dan Dan Noodles
- Baked Ziti with Mozzarella and Ricotta
- Duck Confit Noodles
- Pumpkin Sage Ravioli
- Lobster and Corn Pasta
- Pappardelle with Wild Mushrooms
- Seafood Linguine with Lemon
- Prawn Laksa
- Japanese Yakisoba
- Spaghetti Aglio e Olio
- Black Bean Noodles (Jajangmyeon)
- Grilled Chicken Pad Thai
- Chilled Soba Noodles with Dipping Sauce
- Fettuccine Bolognese

- Lobster Mac and Cheese with Panko Crust
- Duck and Foie Gras Ravioli
- Spaghetti with Clams and White Wine
- Chicken and Mushroom Stroganoff
- Vegan Pad Thai
- Spicy Tuna Poke Noodles
- Truffle Noodle Salad
- Roasted Tomato and Basil Pasta
- Creamy Garlic Parmesan Noodles
- Black Sesame Soba Noodles
- Pappardelle with Veal Ragu
- Spinach and Ricotta Stuffed Shells
- Eggplant Parmesan with Spaghetti
- Thai Green Curry Noodles

Truffle Mac and Cheese

Ingredients:

- 1 lb elbow macaroni
- 2 tbsp butter
- 2 tbsp flour
- 2 cups whole milk
- 1 1/2 cups sharp cheddar cheese (shredded)
- 1 1/2 cups Gruyère cheese (shredded)
- 1/4 cup truffle oil
- Salt and pepper to taste
- 1/2 cup panko breadcrumbs (optional)

Instructions:

1. Cook the macaroni according to package instructions. Drain and set aside.
2. In a large saucepan, melt butter over medium heat. Stir in flour and cook for 1-2 minutes to form a roux.
3. Gradually whisk in the milk and cook until the sauce thickens.
4. Stir in the cheeses until melted and smooth.
5. Add the cooked macaroni and mix until well-coated.
6. Stir in the truffle oil, then season with salt and pepper.
7. Optional: For a crispy topping, sprinkle panko breadcrumbs on top and broil for 2-3 minutes until golden.

Lobster Fettuccine Alfredo

Ingredients:

- 1 lb fettuccine
- 2 tbsp butter
- 2 cloves garlic (minced)
- 1 cup heavy cream
- 1 cup grated Parmesan cheese
- 1/2 cup lobster meat (cooked and chopped)
- 1 tbsp lemon juice
- Salt and pepper to taste

Instructions:

1. Cook the fettuccine according to package instructions. Drain and set aside.
2. In a large skillet, melt butter over medium heat. Add garlic and cook for 1 minute.
3. Pour in the heavy cream and bring to a simmer. Cook for 3-5 minutes until the sauce thickens.
4. Stir in the Parmesan cheese and cook until melted and smooth.
5. Add the lobster meat, lemon juice, and season with salt and pepper.
6. Toss the cooked fettuccine in the sauce and serve immediately.

Thai Pad Thai
Ingredients:

- 8 oz rice noodles
- 2 tbsp vegetable oil
- 1/2 cup shrimp (peeled and deveined)
- 2 eggs (beaten)
- 1 cup bean sprouts
- 2 tbsp fish sauce
- 1 tbsp soy sauce
- 1 tbsp sugar
- 1 tsp chili paste
- 1/4 cup peanuts (chopped)
- 1 lime (cut into wedges)
- Fresh cilantro (for garnish)

Instructions:

1. Cook the rice noodles according to package instructions. Drain and set aside.
2. In a large skillet or wok, heat the oil over medium heat. Add shrimp and cook until pink, about 2-3 minutes.
3. Push the shrimp to one side and scramble the beaten eggs in the pan until cooked through.
4. Add the cooked noodles to the pan and toss.

5. In a small bowl, mix the fish sauce, soy sauce, sugar, and chili paste. Pour over the noodles and toss to coat.

6. Stir in the bean sprouts and cook for another 2 minutes.

7. Serve with chopped peanuts, lime wedges, and cilantro.

Beef Stroganoff with Egg Noodles
Ingredients:

- 1 lb beef tenderloin (cut into thin strips)
- 2 tbsp butter
- 1 onion (chopped)
- 2 cloves garlic (minced)
- 1 cup mushrooms (sliced)
- 1/2 cup beef broth
- 1 cup sour cream
- 2 tbsp Dijon mustard
- Salt and pepper to taste
- 1 lb egg noodles

Instructions:

1. Cook the egg noodles according to package instructions. Drain and set aside.
2. In a large skillet, melt butter over medium heat. Add the beef and cook until browned, about 4-5 minutes.
3. Remove the beef and set aside. In the same skillet, sauté onions and garlic until softened.
4. Add the mushrooms and cook until they release their juices.
5. Pour in the beef broth, bring to a simmer, and cook for 5 minutes.

6. Stir in the sour cream and Dijon mustard. Return the beef to the pan and cook for another 2-3 minutes.

7. Season with salt and pepper, then serve over egg noodles.

Carbonara with Pancetta
Ingredients:

- 12 oz spaghetti
- 1/2 cup pancetta (diced)
- 2 eggs (beaten)
- 1/2 cup Parmesan cheese (grated)
- 1/4 cup pecorino Romano cheese (grated)
- Salt and pepper to taste

Instructions:

1. Cook the spaghetti according to package instructions. Reserve 1 cup of pasta water and drain the noodles.
2. In a large skillet, cook the pancetta over medium heat until crispy, about 4-5 minutes.
3. In a bowl, whisk together the eggs, Parmesan, and pecorino. Season with salt and pepper.
4. Add the cooked pasta to the skillet with pancetta and toss to combine.
5. Remove from heat and slowly pour the egg mixture over the pasta, tossing quickly to create a creamy sauce.
6. Add pasta water, a little at a time, to reach your desired consistency. Serve immediately.

Miso Ramen with Soft-Boiled Egg

Ingredients:

- 4 cups chicken broth
- 2 tbsp miso paste
- 2 tbsp soy sauce
- 1 tbsp sesame oil
- 2 garlic cloves (minced)
- 2 eggs (soft-boiled)
- 2 servings ramen noodles
- 1/2 cup green onions (chopped)
- 1/2 cup nori (seaweed)
- 1/2 cup mushrooms (sliced)
- 1 tsp chili oil (optional)

Instructions:

1. In a large pot, bring the chicken broth to a simmer. Stir in the miso paste, soy sauce, sesame oil, and garlic.
2. Cook the ramen noodles according to package instructions. Drain and set aside.
3. In a separate pot, bring water to a boil and cook the eggs for 7 minutes for soft-boiled eggs. Peel and set aside.
4. Add the cooked noodles to the broth and simmer for another 2-3 minutes.
5. Divide the noodles into bowls and ladle the broth over them.

6. Top with soft-boiled eggs, green onions, nori, mushrooms, and chili oil. Serve hot.

Lobster Bisque Noodles

Ingredients:

- 1 lb lobster meat (cooked and chopped)
- 1 lb fettuccine or tagliatelle
- 2 tbsp butter
- 1 onion (chopped)
- 2 cloves garlic (minced)
- 1 cup heavy cream
- 2 cups lobster broth (or chicken broth)
- 1/4 cup brandy (optional)
- 1/2 tsp paprika
- Salt and pepper to taste

Instructions:

1. Cook the pasta according to package instructions. Drain and set aside.
2. In a large skillet, melt butter over medium heat. Add the onion and garlic and cook until softened.
3. Stir in the lobster broth and bring to a simmer.
4. If using brandy, add it now and cook for 2 minutes to cook off the alcohol.
5. Stir in the cream, paprika, and lobster meat. Cook for another 2-3 minutes.
6. Season with salt and pepper, then toss the cooked noodles into the sauce. Serve warm.

Shrimp Scampi with Linguine
Ingredients:

- 1 lb linguine
- 1 lb shrimp (peeled and deveined)
- 4 tbsp butter
- 2 tbsp olive oil
- 3 garlic cloves (minced)
- 1/2 tsp red pepper flakes
- 1/2 cup white wine
- 1 tbsp lemon juice
- Fresh parsley (chopped)
- Salt and pepper to taste

Instructions:

1. Cook the linguine according to package instructions. Drain and set aside.
2. In a large skillet, heat butter and olive oil over medium heat. Add the shrimp and cook for 2-3 minutes per side until pink.
3. Add garlic and red pepper flakes, cooking for 1 minute until fragrant.
4. Pour in the white wine and lemon juice, stirring to combine. Let the sauce simmer for 2-3 minutes.
5. Add the cooked linguine to the skillet, tossing to coat.
6. Season with salt, pepper, and chopped parsley. Serve immediately.

Butternut Squash Ravioli

Ingredients:

- 1 package fresh or homemade ravioli (filled with butternut squash)
- 2 tbsp butter
- 2 sage leaves (fresh)
- 1/4 cup Parmesan cheese (grated)
- Salt and pepper to taste
- 1/4 cup walnuts (toasted, optional)

Instructions:

1. Cook the ravioli according to package instructions.
2. In a skillet, melt butter over medium heat. Add the sage leaves and cook until the butter begins to brown and become fragrant, about 2-3 minutes.
3. Toss the cooked ravioli in the brown butter sauce.
4. Sprinkle with Parmesan cheese and toasted walnuts (if using).
5. Season with salt and pepper and serve immediately.

Peking Duck Noodles

Ingredients:

- 2 cups cooked Peking duck (shredded)
- 1 package egg noodles (or your preferred noodle)
- 1/4 cup hoisin sauce
- 1 tbsp soy sauce
- 1 tbsp rice vinegar
- 1 tsp sesame oil
- 1/4 cup cucumber (julienned)
- 1/4 cup scallions (chopped)
- 1 tsp sesame seeds (optional)

Instructions:

1. Cook the noodles according to package instructions. Drain and set aside.
2. In a separate skillet, heat hoisin sauce, soy sauce, rice vinegar, and sesame oil over medium heat.
3. Add the shredded Peking duck and stir to coat it with the sauce.
4. Toss the cooked noodles in the sauce and duck mixture.
5. Garnish with julienned cucumber, chopped scallions, and sesame seeds. Serve warm.

Szechuan Noodles

Ingredients:

- 8 oz noodles (your choice)
- 2 tbsp vegetable oil
- 2 cloves garlic (minced)
- 1 tbsp ginger (grated)
- 2 tbsp soy sauce
- 1 tbsp Szechuan peppercorns (crushed)
- 1 tbsp chili paste
- 1 tbsp rice vinegar
- 1 tbsp sesame oil
- 1/4 cup green onions (chopped)
- 1 tbsp roasted peanuts (chopped)

Instructions:

1. Cook the noodles according to package instructions. Drain and set aside.
2. In a large skillet, heat vegetable oil over medium heat. Add garlic and ginger, sautéing for 1-2 minutes.
3. Stir in soy sauce, Szechuan peppercorns, chili paste, rice vinegar, and sesame oil. Bring to a simmer.
4. Toss the cooked noodles in the sauce, stirring to coat.
5. Garnish with chopped green onions and roasted peanuts. Serve immediately.

Sweet Potato Gnocchi

Ingredients:

- 1 lb sweet potatoes (peeled and mashed)
- 1 egg
- 1 cup flour (more for dusting)
- 1/2 tsp salt
- 1/4 tsp nutmeg
- 1 tbsp butter
- 1/4 cup sage leaves (fresh)

Instructions:

1. Boil the sweet potatoes until soft, then mash them. Allow them to cool.
2. In a mixing bowl, combine the mashed sweet potatoes, egg, flour, salt, and nutmeg to form a dough.
3. Roll the dough into long ropes, then cut into bite-sized pieces. Use a fork to create ridges on each gnocchi.
4. Boil the gnocchi in salted water until they float to the top, about 2-3 minutes.
5. In a skillet, melt butter over medium heat. Add the sage leaves and cook for 1-2 minutes until fragrant.
6. Toss the gnocchi in the butter-sage sauce and serve warm.

Braised Pork Belly Ramen

Ingredients:

- 2 cups pork belly (cut into slices)
- 4 cups chicken broth
- 2 tbsp soy sauce
- 1 tbsp hoisin sauce
- 1 tbsp rice vinegar
- 2 tbsp brown sugar
- 2 servings ramen noodles
- 2 boiled eggs (soft-boiled)
- 1/4 cup green onions (chopped)
- 1 tsp chili oil (optional)

Instructions:

1. In a large pot, combine chicken broth, soy sauce, hoisin sauce, rice vinegar, and brown sugar. Bring to a simmer.
2. Add the pork belly slices to the pot and braise for about 1 hour, until tender.
3. Cook the ramen noodles according to package instructions. Drain and set aside.
4. Once the pork is tender, remove from the broth and slice it thinly.
5. Serve the ramen noodles in bowls, topping with braised pork, boiled eggs, green onions, and chili oil (optional).

Garlic Butter Shrimp Pasta

Ingredients:

- 8 oz pasta (linguine or spaghetti)
- 1 lb shrimp (peeled and deveined)
- 4 tbsp butter
- 4 cloves garlic (minced)
- 1/4 tsp red pepper flakes
- 1/4 cup fresh parsley (chopped)
- 1 tbsp lemon juice
- Salt and pepper to taste

Instructions:

1. Cook the pasta according to package instructions. Drain and set aside.
2. In a large skillet, melt butter over medium heat. Add garlic and red pepper flakes, cooking for 1-2 minutes.
3. Add shrimp and cook for 3-4 minutes until pink and cooked through.
4. Toss the cooked pasta in the garlic butter shrimp mixture.
5. Add lemon juice and fresh parsley, season with salt and pepper. Serve immediately.

Tofu and Veggie Stir-Fry Noodles

Ingredients:

- 1 block firm tofu (pressed and cubed)
- 2 cups mixed vegetables (bell peppers, broccoli, carrots, etc.)
- 2 tbsp soy sauce
- 1 tbsp rice vinegar
- 1 tbsp sesame oil
- 1 tbsp hoisin sauce
- 8 oz noodles (your choice)
- 1 tbsp sesame seeds (optional)
- 2 green onions (chopped)

Instructions:

1. Cook the noodles according to package instructions. Drain and set aside.
2. In a large skillet, heat sesame oil over medium heat. Add tofu and cook until golden brown, about 5-7 minutes.
3. Remove the tofu and set aside. In the same skillet, sauté the vegetables until tender.
4. Add soy sauce, rice vinegar, and hoisin sauce to the vegetables, cooking for 2-3 minutes.
5. Toss in the cooked noodles and tofu, mixing well.
6. Garnish with sesame seeds and chopped green onions. Serve warm.

Zucchini Noodles with Pesto

Ingredients:

- 2 large zucchinis (spiralized into noodles)
- 1/2 cup pesto sauce (store-bought or homemade)
- 1 tbsp olive oil
- 1/4 cup Parmesan cheese (shredded)
- Salt and pepper to taste

Instructions:

1. In a skillet, heat olive oil over medium heat. Add the zucchini noodles and sauté for 2-3 minutes until tender.
2. Toss the zucchini noodles in pesto sauce, mixing until well coated.
3. Season with salt and pepper.
4. Serve topped with shredded Parmesan cheese.

Braised Short Rib Pasta

Ingredients:

- 2 lbs short ribs
- 1 tbsp olive oil
- 1 onion (chopped)
- 2 carrots (chopped)
- 2 celery stalks (chopped)
- 4 cloves garlic (minced)
- 2 cups red wine
- 4 cups beef broth
- 1 tbsp tomato paste
- 2 bay leaves
- 1 tsp thyme
- Salt and pepper to taste
- 1 lb pasta (penne or rigatoni)
- Fresh parsley (chopped, for garnish)

Instructions:

1. Preheat the oven to 350°F (175°C).
2. Heat olive oil in a large oven-safe pot over medium-high heat. Brown the short ribs on all sides, about 6-8 minutes. Remove and set aside.

3. Add onion, carrots, celery, and garlic to the pot, cooking for 5 minutes until softened.

4. Stir in tomato paste, then pour in red wine and beef broth. Add bay leaves and thyme.

5. Return short ribs to the pot, cover, and braise in the oven for 2.5-3 hours, until the meat is tender and falling off the bone.

6. Remove the short ribs, discard the bones, and shred the meat.

7. Cook the pasta according to package instructions. Drain and toss with the braised short rib sauce.

8. Serve with fresh parsley on top.

Green Curry Noodles

Ingredients:

- 8 oz rice noodles
- 1 tbsp vegetable oil
- 1 tbsp green curry paste
- 1 can (14 oz) coconut milk
- 1 tbsp soy sauce
- 1 tbsp brown sugar
- 1 red bell pepper (sliced)
- 1/2 cup baby spinach
- 1/4 cup fresh basil (chopped)
- 1 tbsp lime juice
- 1/4 cup peanuts (chopped, for garnish)
- Chili flakes (optional)

Instructions:

1. Cook the rice noodles according to package instructions. Drain and set aside.
2. Heat vegetable oil in a skillet over medium heat. Add green curry paste and cook for 1-2 minutes until fragrant.
3. Pour in the coconut milk, soy sauce, and brown sugar, stirring to combine. Simmer for 5-7 minutes until the sauce thickens slightly.
4. Add the bell pepper and spinach to the sauce, cooking for another 2 minutes.

5. Toss the cooked noodles in the curry sauce, then add lime juice and fresh basil.

6. Serve garnished with chopped peanuts and chili flakes.

Truffle Macaroni

Ingredients:

- 8 oz macaroni pasta
- 2 tbsp butter
- 1/2 cup heavy cream
- 1/2 cup grated Parmesan cheese
- 1/4 cup truffle oil
- 1/2 tsp garlic powder
- Salt and pepper to taste
- Fresh parsley (chopped, for garnish)

Instructions:

1. Cook the macaroni pasta according to package instructions. Drain and set aside.
2. In a saucepan, melt butter over medium heat. Add heavy cream and bring to a simmer.
3. Stir in Parmesan cheese, garlic powder, salt, and pepper, cooking until the cheese has melted and the sauce is smooth.
4. Add the cooked macaroni to the sauce, tossing to coat.
5. Drizzle with truffle oil and garnish with fresh parsley. Serve warm.

Pad See Ew
Ingredients:

- 8 oz wide rice noodles
- 2 tbsp vegetable oil
- 1 chicken breast (sliced)
- 2 eggs
- 2 garlic cloves (minced)
- 1 cup broccoli florets
- 2 tbsp soy sauce
- 1 tbsp oyster sauce
- 1 tbsp dark soy sauce
- 1 tsp sugar
- 1/2 tsp white pepper
- Lime wedges (for serving)

Instructions:

1. Cook the rice noodles according to package instructions. Drain and set aside.
2. Heat vegetable oil in a large skillet or wok over medium-high heat. Add chicken slices and cook until browned, about 5-7 minutes. Remove and set aside.
3. In the same skillet, scramble the eggs. Once cooked, push them to one side of the skillet.
4. Add garlic and broccoli, stir-frying for 2-3 minutes until tender.

5. Add the cooked noodles, soy sauce, oyster sauce, dark soy sauce, sugar, and white pepper. Toss everything together.

6. Add the cooked chicken back into the skillet and stir to combine.

7. Serve with lime wedges for extra flavor.

Korean Japchae (Stir-Fried Glass Noodles)
Ingredients:

- 8 oz glass noodles (dangmyeon)
- 2 tbsp vegetable oil
- 1/2 lb beef (thinly sliced)
- 1 onion (sliced)
- 1 carrot (julienned)
- 1/2 red bell pepper (sliced)
- 2 cups spinach
- 2 tbsp soy sauce
- 1 tbsp sesame oil
- 1 tbsp sugar
- 1 tbsp garlic (minced)
- 1 tbsp sesame seeds
- 2 green onions (chopped)

Instructions:

1. Cook the glass noodles according to package instructions. Drain and set aside.
2. In a large skillet, heat vegetable oil over medium heat. Add the beef and cook until browned, about 5 minutes. Remove and set aside.
3. In the same skillet, add onion, carrot, and bell pepper. Stir-fry for 3-4 minutes until tender.

4. Add spinach and cook until wilted.

5. Add the cooked noodles, soy sauce, sesame oil, sugar, and garlic. Toss everything together for 2-3 minutes.

6. Stir in the cooked beef, sesame seeds, and green onions.

7. Serve warm.

Beef and Broccoli Udon

Ingredients:

- 8 oz udon noodles
- 1 lb beef (sliced thinly)
- 1 tbsp vegetable oil
- 2 cups broccoli florets
- 3 tbsp soy sauce
- 1 tbsp oyster sauce
- 1 tbsp brown sugar
- 1 tsp garlic (minced)
- 1 tsp ginger (grated)
- 1 tbsp sesame oil

Instructions:

1. Cook the udon noodles according to package instructions. Drain and set aside.
2. In a large skillet, heat vegetable oil over medium heat. Add the beef and cook for 3-4 minutes until browned.
3. Add broccoli florets and cook for an additional 2-3 minutes.
4. Stir in soy sauce, oyster sauce, brown sugar, garlic, and ginger, cooking for 1-2 minutes until the sauce thickens slightly.
5. Toss the cooked udon noodles into the skillet and drizzle with sesame oil.
6. Serve warm.

Spicy Szechuan Dan Dan Noodles

Ingredients:

- 8 oz noodles (your choice)
- 1 tbsp vegetable oil
- 1/2 lb ground pork
- 2 tbsp Szechuan peppercorns (crushed)
- 2 tbsp soy sauce
- 2 tbsp sesame paste
- 1 tbsp chili paste
- 1 tbsp rice vinegar
- 1 tbsp sugar
- 1/4 cup green onions (chopped)
- 1 tbsp peanuts (chopped)

Instructions:

1. Cook the noodles according to package instructions. Drain and set aside.
2. In a skillet, heat vegetable oil over medium heat. Add ground pork and cook until browned, about 5 minutes.
3. Add crushed Szechuan peppercorns and cook for another minute until fragrant.
4. Stir in soy sauce, sesame paste, chili paste, rice vinegar, and sugar. Simmer for 2-3 minutes.
5. Toss the cooked noodles in the sauce and pork mixture.

6. Serve with chopped green onions and peanuts.

Baked Ziti with Mozzarella and Ricotta

Ingredients:

- 1 lb ziti pasta
- 2 cups marinara sauce
- 1 cup ricotta cheese
- 2 cups mozzarella cheese (shredded)
- 1/4 cup Parmesan cheese (grated)
- 2 tbsp fresh basil (chopped)
- Salt and pepper to taste

Instructions:

1. Preheat the oven to 375°F (190°C).
2. Cook the ziti pasta according to package instructions. Drain and set aside.
3. In a large mixing bowl, combine ricotta cheese, 1 cup mozzarella, Parmesan cheese, and basil. Season with salt and pepper.
4. Mix the cooked ziti with marinara sauce, then fold in the cheese mixture.
5. Transfer everything to a baking dish and top with the remaining mozzarella.
6. Bake for 25-30 minutes until bubbly and golden brown on top.
7. Serve warm.

Duck Confit Noodles

Ingredients:

- 4 duck leg confit (pre-cooked)
- 8 oz egg noodles
- 1 tbsp olive oil
- 2 cloves garlic (minced)
- 1/2 onion (sliced)
- 1/2 cup dry white wine
- 1/2 cup chicken broth
- 1 tbsp soy sauce
- 1 tbsp fresh thyme
- 1 tbsp fresh parsley (chopped)
- Salt and pepper to taste

Instructions:

1. Cook the egg noodles according to package instructions. Drain and set aside.
2. In a large skillet, heat olive oil over medium heat. Add garlic and onion, cooking until fragrant, about 2-3 minutes.
3. Shred the duck confit meat off the bone and add to the skillet. Cook for 5 minutes until heated through.
4. Pour in the white wine and chicken broth, stirring to combine. Add soy sauce, thyme, salt, and pepper. Simmer for 5 minutes until the sauce has reduced.

5. Toss the cooked noodles into the skillet and stir to coat evenly.

6. Garnish with fresh parsley and serve.

Pumpkin Sage Ravioli

Ingredients:

- 12 oz ravioli (filled with pumpkin)
- 3 tbsp butter
- 10 fresh sage leaves
- 1/4 tsp nutmeg
- 1/2 cup grated Parmesan cheese
- Salt and pepper to taste

Instructions:

1. Cook the pumpkin ravioli according to package instructions. Drain and set aside.
2. In a skillet, melt butter over medium heat. Add fresh sage leaves and cook until crispy, about 2 minutes.
3. Stir in nutmeg and season with salt and pepper.
4. Toss the cooked ravioli in the sage butter sauce, coating them evenly.
5. Sprinkle with Parmesan cheese and serve.

Lobster and Corn Pasta

Ingredients:

- 8 oz linguine or spaghetti
- 2 lobster tails (cooked and chopped)
- 1 cup fresh corn kernels (or frozen, thawed)
- 2 tbsp butter
- 2 cloves garlic (minced)
- 1/2 cup heavy cream
- 1 tbsp lemon juice
- Salt and pepper to taste
- Fresh parsley (chopped, for garnish)

Instructions:

1. Cook the pasta according to package instructions. Drain and set aside.
2. In a large skillet, melt butter over medium heat. Add garlic and cook until fragrant, about 1 minute.
3. Add corn and cook for 3-4 minutes until tender.
4. Stir in the lobster meat, heavy cream, and lemon juice. Cook for another 2-3 minutes, allowing the sauce to thicken slightly.
5. Toss the cooked pasta in the skillet, mixing until well coated.
6. Season with salt and pepper, and garnish with fresh parsley. Serve warm.

Pappardelle with Wild Mushrooms
Ingredients:

- 8 oz pappardelle pasta
- 2 tbsp olive oil
- 1 lb wild mushrooms (such as chanterelles, shiitake, or cremini), sliced
- 2 cloves garlic (minced)
- 1/4 cup white wine
- 1/2 cup heavy cream
- 1/4 cup grated Parmesan cheese
- Fresh thyme (for garnish)
- Salt and pepper to taste

Instructions:

1. Cook the pappardelle pasta according to package instructions. Drain and set aside.
2. In a large skillet, heat olive oil over medium-high heat. Add the mushrooms and cook for 5-7 minutes, until they begin to release their moisture and brown.
3. Add garlic and cook for 1-2 minutes until fragrant.
4. Pour in white wine and let it reduce by half, about 3 minutes.
5. Stir in the heavy cream, and cook for 2-3 minutes until the sauce thickens.
6. Toss the cooked pappardelle into the skillet, coating the pasta with the mushroom sauce.

7. Sprinkle with Parmesan cheese, garnish with thyme, and serve.

Seafood Linguine with Lemon

Ingredients:

- 8 oz linguine
- 2 tbsp olive oil
- 1/2 lb shrimp (peeled and deveined)
- 1/2 lb scallops
- 2 cloves garlic (minced)
- 1/2 cup white wine
- 1/4 cup lemon juice
- 1 tbsp lemon zest
- Salt and pepper to taste
- Fresh parsley (chopped, for garnish)

Instructions:

1. Cook the linguine according to package instructions. Drain and set aside.
2. Heat olive oil in a large skillet over medium heat. Add shrimp and scallops, cooking until opaque, about 3-4 minutes. Remove from the skillet and set aside.
3. In the same skillet, add garlic and cook for 1 minute until fragrant.
4. Pour in white wine and lemon juice, letting the sauce reduce for 2 minutes.
5. Return the shrimp and scallops to the skillet, then add lemon zest and season with salt and pepper.
6. Toss the cooked linguine in the seafood sauce.

7. Garnish with fresh parsley and serve.

Prawn Laksa

Ingredients:

- 8 oz rice noodles
- 2 tbsp red curry paste
- 1 can (14 oz) coconut milk
- 2 cups chicken or vegetable broth
- 1 tbsp fish sauce
- 1 tbsp sugar
- 1/2 lb prawns (peeled and deveined)
- 2 boiled eggs (halved)
- 1/4 cup bean sprouts
- 1/4 cup fresh cilantro (chopped)
- 1 lime (cut into wedges)

Instructions:

1. Cook the rice noodles according to package instructions. Drain and set aside.
2. In a large pot, bring the coconut milk, broth, red curry paste, fish sauce, and sugar to a simmer. Stir until the curry paste is dissolved and the soup base is fragrant.
3. Add prawns to the pot and cook for 2-3 minutes until pink and cooked through.
4. Divide the cooked noodles between bowls and pour the soup over them.
5. Garnish with boiled eggs, bean sprouts, cilantro, and lime wedges. Serve hot.

Japanese Yakisoba

Ingredients:

- 8 oz yakisoba noodles (or substitute with ramen noodles)
- 2 tbsp vegetable oil
- 1/2 lb pork (thinly sliced)
- 1 onion (sliced)
- 1/2 bell pepper (sliced)
- 1 carrot (julienned)
- 1/4 cup soy sauce
- 1 tbsp oyster sauce
- 1 tbsp Worcestershire sauce
- 1 tsp sugar
- 1 tbsp sesame oil
- Green onions (chopped, for garnish)

Instructions:

1. Cook the yakisoba noodles according to package instructions. Drain and set aside.
2. Heat vegetable oil in a large skillet or wok over medium heat. Add pork and cook until browned.
3. Add onion, bell pepper, and carrot, stir-frying for 3-4 minutes until tender.

4. In a small bowl, combine soy sauce, oyster sauce, Worcestershire sauce, and sugar. Pour over the vegetables and pork.

5. Add the cooked noodles, tossing everything together to combine.

6. Drizzle with sesame oil and garnish with chopped green onions. Serve warm.

Spaghetti Aglio e Olio

Ingredients:

- 8 oz spaghetti
- 1/4 cup olive oil
- 6 cloves garlic (sliced thinly)
- 1/2 tsp red pepper flakes
- Salt to taste
- Fresh parsley (chopped, for garnish)
- Freshly grated Parmesan cheese (optional)

Instructions:

1. Cook the spaghetti according to package instructions. Drain, reserving 1/2 cup pasta water.
2. In a large skillet, heat olive oil over medium heat. Add the garlic and cook until golden brown, about 2-3 minutes.
3. Add the red pepper flakes and stir.
4. Toss the cooked spaghetti in the garlic oil, adding a bit of reserved pasta water to help coat the noodles.
5. Season with salt and garnish with parsley. Optionally, top with Parmesan cheese. Serve immediately.

Black Bean Noodles (Jajangmyeon)
Ingredients:

- 8 oz jajangmyeon noodles (or any thick wheat noodles)
- 1/2 lb pork belly or beef (cut into bite-sized cubes)
- 1/2 onion (diced)
- 1 zucchini (julienned)
- 1/2 cup potato (peeled and diced)
- 2 tbsp vegetable oil
- 3 tbsp black bean paste (chunjang)
- 1 tbsp soy sauce
- 1 tsp sugar
- 2 cups chicken or vegetable broth
- 1 tbsp cornstarch (mixed with 2 tbsp water)
- Salt and pepper to taste
- Sliced cucumber (for garnish)

Instructions:

1. Cook the noodles according to package instructions. Drain and set aside.
2. Heat vegetable oil in a large pan or wok over medium-high heat. Add pork (or beef) and cook until browned.
3. Add the onion, zucchini, and potato, cooking for about 5-7 minutes until the vegetables are softened.

4. Stir in the black bean paste, soy sauce, and sugar, and cook for 1-2 minutes.

5. Pour in the broth and bring to a boil. Reduce to a simmer and cook for 10 minutes until the sauce thickens.

6. Stir in the cornstarch mixture and continue cooking for another 2 minutes until the sauce is glossy.

7. Toss the cooked noodles in the sauce, mixing well.

8. Garnish with sliced cucumber and serve immediately.

Grilled Chicken Pad Thai

Ingredients:

- 8 oz rice noodles
- 2 chicken breasts (boneless, skinless)
- 2 tbsp vegetable oil
- 2 cloves garlic (minced)
- 1/4 cup tamarind paste
- 2 tbsp fish sauce
- 1 tbsp soy sauce
- 1 tbsp sugar
- 1/2 cup bean sprouts
- 2 eggs (beaten)
- 1/4 cup roasted peanuts (chopped)
- 1 lime (cut into wedges)
- Fresh cilantro (for garnish)

Instructions:

1. Cook the rice noodles according to package instructions. Drain and set aside.
2. Preheat the grill to medium-high heat. Season the chicken breasts with salt, pepper, and a little oil. Grill for 6-8 minutes per side, until cooked through. Slice thinly.

3. In a large skillet, heat oil over medium heat. Add garlic and cook until fragrant, about 1 minute.

4. Stir in the tamarind paste, fish sauce, soy sauce, and sugar. Cook for 2-3 minutes, stirring to dissolve the sugar.

5. Push the sauce mixture to one side of the skillet and pour the beaten eggs into the other side. Scramble the eggs until cooked, then mix with the sauce.

6. Add the cooked noodles and toss to coat in the sauce.

7. Top with grilled chicken, bean sprouts, peanuts, and fresh cilantro. Serve with lime wedges on the side.

Chilled Soba Noodles with Dipping Sauce
Ingredients:

- 8 oz soba noodles
- 2 cups dashi broth
- 1/4 cup soy sauce
- 2 tbsp mirin
- 1 tbsp rice vinegar
- 1 tsp sugar
- 1/4 tsp sesame oil
- 1 scallion (sliced thinly)
- 1 tbsp toasted sesame seeds

Instructions:

1. Cook the soba noodles according to package instructions. Drain and rinse with cold water to chill the noodles. Set aside.

2. In a small saucepan, combine dashi broth, soy sauce, mirin, rice vinegar, sugar, and sesame oil. Bring to a simmer over medium heat, stirring to dissolve the sugar. Let cool to room temperature.

3. To serve, place the chilled soba noodles in a bowl. Pour the dipping sauce into small bowls for dipping.

4. Garnish with sliced scallions and sesame seeds. Serve immediately.

Fettuccine Bolognese

Ingredients:

- 8 oz fettuccine pasta
- 1/2 lb ground beef
- 1/2 lb ground pork
- 1 onion (chopped)
- 2 cloves garlic (minced)
- 1 carrot (chopped)
- 2 tbsp tomato paste
- 1 cup crushed tomatoes
- 1/2 cup red wine
- 1 cup whole milk
- 1 tsp dried oregano
- Salt and pepper to taste
- Fresh parsley (for garnish)
- Grated Parmesan cheese (for serving)

Instructions:

1. Cook the fettuccine pasta according to package instructions. Drain and set aside.

2. In a large skillet, heat oil over medium-high heat. Add the ground beef and pork, breaking it up with a spoon as it cooks. Cook until browned.

3. Add the onion, garlic, and carrot. Cook until softened, about 5 minutes.

4. Stir in the tomato paste and cook for 2 minutes. Add the crushed tomatoes, red wine, and dried oregano. Bring to a simmer and cook for 30 minutes, stirring occasionally.

5. Stir in the milk and cook for an additional 10 minutes, allowing the sauce to thicken. Season with salt and pepper.

6. Toss the cooked fettuccine in the Bolognese sauce.

7. Garnish with fresh parsley and grated Parmesan cheese. Serve warm.

Lobster Mac and Cheese with Panko Crust

Ingredients:

- 8 oz elbow macaroni
- 2 lobster tails (cooked and chopped)
- 2 tbsp butter
- 2 tbsp flour
- 2 cups whole milk
- 2 cups shredded sharp cheddar cheese
- 1 cup grated Gruyère cheese
- 1/2 cup panko breadcrumbs
- 1 tbsp melted butter
- Salt and pepper to taste
- Fresh parsley (for garnish)

Instructions:

1. Cook the elbow macaroni according to package instructions. Drain and set aside.

2. In a large saucepan, melt butter over medium heat. Add flour and cook for 1-2 minutes, stirring constantly to form a roux.

3. Gradually add the milk, whisking to combine. Cook until the sauce thickens, about 5 minutes.

4. Stir in the shredded cheddar and Gruyère cheese until melted and smooth. Season with salt and pepper.

5. Gently fold in the cooked lobster and pasta.

6. Preheat the oven to 375°F (190°C). Transfer the mac and cheese to a baking dish.

7. In a small bowl, combine panko breadcrumbs and melted butter. Sprinkle over the mac and cheese.

8. Bake for 20-25 minutes, until the top is golden and crispy.

9. Garnish with fresh parsley and serve.

Duck and Foie Gras Ravioli

Ingredients:

- 8 oz fresh ravioli (store-bought or homemade with duck and foie gras filling)
- 2 tbsp butter
- 1 tbsp olive oil
- 1/2 cup chicken broth
- 1/4 cup heavy cream
- 1 tbsp fresh thyme (chopped)
- Salt and pepper to taste
- Grated Parmesan (for serving)

Instructions:

1. Cook the ravioli according to package instructions. Drain and set aside.
2. In a large skillet, heat butter and olive oil over medium heat.
3. Add the chicken broth and bring to a simmer. Stir in the heavy cream and thyme. Let cook for 2-3 minutes until the sauce thickens slightly.
4. Season with salt and pepper.
5. Gently toss the cooked ravioli in the sauce, coating them evenly.
6. Serve with a sprinkle of grated Parmesan cheese and fresh thyme.

Spaghetti with Clams and White Wine

Ingredients:

- 8 oz spaghetti
- 2 tbsp olive oil
- 2 cloves garlic (minced)
- 1/2 tsp red pepper flakes (optional)
- 2 dozen fresh clams (scrubbed)
- 1 cup white wine
- 1/4 cup chopped parsley
- 1 tbsp lemon juice
- Salt and pepper to taste

Instructions:

1. Cook the spaghetti according to package instructions. Drain and set aside, reserving 1/2 cup of pasta water.
2. Heat olive oil in a large skillet over medium heat. Add garlic and red pepper flakes (if using), cooking until fragrant, about 1 minute.
3. Add the clams and white wine to the skillet. Cover and cook for 5-7 minutes, until the clams have opened.
4. Discard any unopened clams.
5. Toss the cooked spaghetti in the skillet with the clams, adding reserved pasta water as needed to create a smooth sauce.
6. Stir in parsley, lemon juice, salt, and pepper. Serve immediately.

Chicken and Mushroom Stroganoff

Ingredients:

- 2 chicken breasts (boneless, skinless, cut into strips)
- 1 tbsp olive oil
- 8 oz mushrooms (sliced)
- 1 onion (diced)
- 2 cloves garlic (minced)
- 1/2 cup white wine
- 1 cup chicken broth
- 1 tbsp flour
- 1/2 cup sour cream
- 1 tbsp Dijon mustard
- Salt and pepper to taste
- Fresh parsley (for garnish)

Instructions:

1. Heat olive oil in a large skillet over medium heat. Add chicken strips and cook until browned and cooked through, about 5-7 minutes. Remove and set aside.

2. In the same skillet, add mushrooms, onion, and garlic, cooking until softened, about 5 minutes.

3. Sprinkle flour over the mushrooms and stir to combine.

4. Pour in the white wine and chicken broth, stirring until the sauce thickens, about 5 minutes.

5. Stir in the sour cream and Dijon mustard. Return the chicken to the skillet and cook for 2-3 minutes to heat through.

6. Season with salt and pepper and garnish with parsley. Serve over egg noodles or rice.

Vegan Pad Thai

Ingredients:

- 8 oz rice noodles
- 1 tbsp vegetable oil
- 1/2 onion (sliced)
- 2 cloves garlic (minced)
- 1/2 cup shredded carrots
- 1/2 cup bell pepper (julienned)
- 1/2 cup snap peas (sliced)
- 1/4 cup tamarind paste
- 2 tbsp soy sauce (or tamari for gluten-free)
- 1 tbsp maple syrup or agave
- 1 tbsp lime juice
- 1 tbsp peanut butter (optional)
- 1/4 cup roasted peanuts (chopped, for garnish)
- Fresh cilantro (for garnish)
- Lime wedges (for serving)

Instructions:

1. Cook the rice noodles according to package instructions. Drain and set aside.

2. Heat the oil in a large pan or wok over medium heat. Add the onion and garlic and sauté for 2 minutes until fragrant.

3. Add the shredded carrots, bell pepper, and snap peas, and cook for another 3-4 minutes until softened.

4. In a small bowl, whisk together the tamarind paste, soy sauce, maple syrup, lime juice, and peanut butter (if using). Add the sauce to the pan with the vegetables.

5. Toss the cooked noodles into the pan and stir to combine with the sauce and veggies.

6. Garnish with chopped peanuts and fresh cilantro. Serve with lime wedges.

Spicy Tuna Poke Noodles

Ingredients:

- 8 oz udon noodles (or any noodles of choice)
- 1/2 lb sushi-grade tuna (diced)
- 1/4 cup soy sauce
- 1 tbsp sriracha sauce (adjust for spice)
- 1 tbsp sesame oil
- 1 tbsp rice vinegar
- 1 tbsp honey or maple syrup
- 1/4 tsp garlic powder
- 1/4 tsp ginger powder
- 1/2 avocado (sliced)
- 1/4 cup cucumber (julienned)
- 1/4 cup scallions (chopped)
- 1 tbsp sesame seeds (for garnish)
- Seaweed (for garnish, optional)

Instructions:

1. Cook the noodles according to package instructions. Drain and set aside.
2. In a bowl, combine the soy sauce, sriracha sauce, sesame oil, rice vinegar, honey, garlic powder, and ginger powder to make the sauce.

3. Add the diced tuna to the sauce and toss to coat. Let it marinate for 5-10 minutes.

4. Arrange the noodles in serving bowls. Top with the spicy tuna mixture, sliced avocado, cucumber, and scallions.

5. Garnish with sesame seeds and seaweed, if using.

Truffle Noodle Salad

Ingredients:

- 8 oz spaghetti or other pasta of choice
- 1/4 cup olive oil
- 1 tbsp truffle oil (or more to taste)
- 1/4 cup Parmesan (vegan Parmesan optional)
- 1/4 cup fresh parsley (chopped)
- 1/4 cup toasted pine nuts (optional)
- Salt and pepper to taste
- Lemon zest (optional)

Instructions:

1. Cook the pasta according to package instructions. Drain and let it cool to room temperature.
2. In a large bowl, combine the olive oil and truffle oil.
3. Toss the cooked pasta with the oil mixture. Add in the Parmesan (or vegan Parmesan) and mix well.
4. Add the fresh parsley, pine nuts (if using), salt, and pepper. Toss again.
5. For extra flavor, top with lemon zest.
6. Serve chilled or at room temperature.

Roasted Tomato and Basil Pasta

Ingredients:

- 8 oz penne or spaghetti
- 1 pint cherry tomatoes (halved)
- 1 tbsp olive oil
- 2 cloves garlic (minced)
- Salt and pepper to taste
- 1/4 cup fresh basil (chopped)
- 1 tbsp balsamic vinegar (optional)
- 1/4 cup Parmesan cheese (optional)

Instructions:

1. Preheat the oven to 400°F (200°C).
2. Toss the halved tomatoes with olive oil, minced garlic, salt, and pepper. Spread them on a baking sheet in a single layer.
3. Roast for 20-25 minutes, or until the tomatoes are soft and slightly caramelized.
4. While the tomatoes roast, cook the pasta according to package instructions. Drain and set aside.
5. Once the tomatoes are roasted, toss them with the cooked pasta, fresh basil, and balsamic vinegar (if using).
6. Serve with a sprinkle of Parmesan, if desired.

Creamy Garlic Parmesan Noodles

Ingredients:

- 8 oz fettuccine or linguine
- 2 tbsp butter (or vegan butter)
- 3 cloves garlic (minced)
- 1 cup heavy cream (or coconut cream for dairy-free)
- 1/2 cup grated Parmesan (or vegan Parmesan)
- Salt and pepper to taste
- Fresh parsley (for garnish)

Instructions:

1. Cook the pasta according to package instructions. Drain and set aside.
2. In a large pan, melt butter over medium heat. Add the minced garlic and sauté for 1-2 minutes until fragrant.
3. Add the heavy cream to the pan and simmer for 3-4 minutes, stirring occasionally.
4. Stir in the Parmesan and mix until the sauce is creamy. Season with salt and pepper to taste.
5. Toss the cooked pasta in the creamy garlic sauce until well-coated.
6. Garnish with fresh parsley and serve immediately.

Black Sesame Soba Noodles

Ingredients:

- 8 oz soba noodles
- 2 tbsp black sesame seeds (toasted)
- 2 tbsp sesame oil
- 1 tbsp soy sauce (or tamari for gluten-free)
- 1 tbsp rice vinegar
- 1 tsp honey or agave syrup
- 1 tsp grated ginger
- 1/4 cup sliced scallions
- 1/4 cup cucumber (julienned)
- 1/4 cup cilantro (chopped)
- 1 tbsp toasted sesame oil (for finishing)

Instructions:

1. Cook the soba noodles according to package instructions. Drain and rinse with cold water to stop the cooking process. Set aside.
2. In a small bowl, whisk together the sesame oil, soy sauce, rice vinegar, honey, and grated ginger.
3. Toss the cooled noodles with the sesame sauce.
4. Top with toasted black sesame seeds, sliced scallions, cucumber, and cilantro.

5. Drizzle with toasted sesame oil and serve chilled or at room temperature.

Pappardelle with Veal Ragu

Ingredients:

- 8 oz pappardelle pasta
- 1 lb veal shoulder or veal stew meat (cut into chunks)
- 2 tbsp olive oil
- 1 onion (chopped)
- 2 cloves garlic (minced)
- 2 carrots (diced)
- 1 celery stalk (diced)
- 1/2 cup red wine
- 1 can (14 oz) crushed tomatoes
- 1 cup beef broth (or vegetable broth)
- 1 bay leaf
- 1 tsp dried thyme
- Salt and pepper to taste
- Fresh parsley (for garnish)
- Grated Parmesan cheese (optional)

Instructions:

1. Heat the olive oil in a large pot over medium-high heat. Brown the veal chunks on all sides, then remove them and set aside.

2. In the same pot, add the onion, garlic, carrots, and celery. Cook until softened, about 5 minutes.

3. Pour in the red wine and cook for 2-3 minutes, scraping any brown bits from the bottom of the pot.

4. Add the crushed tomatoes, beef broth, bay leaf, and thyme. Return the veal to the pot. Bring to a simmer.

5. Cover and let the ragu cook for about 1.5 to 2 hours, until the veal is tender and the sauce is rich.

6. Meanwhile, cook the pappardelle pasta according to package instructions. Drain and set aside.

7. Remove the veal from the sauce and shred it with a fork. Return the shredded veal to the pot and stir to combine.

8. Serve the veal ragu over the pappardelle pasta. Garnish with fresh parsley and grated Parmesan, if desired.

Spinach and Ricotta Stuffed Shells

Ingredients:

- 20 jumbo pasta shells
- 1 cup ricotta cheese
- 1 cup fresh spinach (chopped)
- 1 cup shredded mozzarella cheese
- 1/4 cup grated Parmesan cheese
- 1 egg
- 2 cups marinara sauce
- 1 tbsp olive oil
- Salt and pepper to taste
- Fresh basil (for garnish)

Instructions:

1. Preheat the oven to 375°F (190°C).
2. Cook the jumbo pasta shells according to package instructions. Drain and set aside.
3. In a bowl, combine the ricotta cheese, chopped spinach, mozzarella, Parmesan, and egg. Season with salt and pepper.
4. Stuff each pasta shell with the spinach and ricotta mixture.
5. In a baking dish, spread a thin layer of marinara sauce on the bottom. Arrange the stuffed shells on top of the sauce.

6. Pour the remaining marinara sauce over the stuffed shells and sprinkle with additional mozzarella cheese if desired.

7. Cover with aluminum foil and bake for 25-30 minutes, until bubbly.

8. Garnish with fresh basil before serving.

Eggplant Parmesan with Spaghetti

Ingredients:

- 2 medium eggplants (sliced into 1/4-inch thick rounds)
- 1 cup all-purpose flour
- 2 eggs (beaten)
- 2 cups breadcrumbs (preferably panko)
- 1 tbsp dried oregano
- 2 cups marinara sauce
- 1 1/2 cups shredded mozzarella cheese
- 1/4 cup grated Parmesan cheese
- 8 oz spaghetti
- Olive oil for frying
- Salt and pepper to taste
- Fresh basil (for garnish)

Instructions:

1. Preheat the oven to 375°F (190°C).
2. Set up a breading station with three shallow bowls: one with flour, one with beaten eggs, and one with breadcrumbs mixed with dried oregano, salt, and pepper.
3. Dredge each eggplant slice in flour, dip into the egg, and coat with the breadcrumb mixture.

4. Heat olive oil in a large skillet over medium heat. Fry the eggplant slices until golden brown on both sides, about 3-4 minutes per side. Drain on paper towels.

5. In a baking dish, spread a thin layer of marinara sauce. Layer the fried eggplant slices, then top with more sauce and mozzarella cheese.

6. Repeat the layers until all eggplant is used. Top with grated Parmesan cheese.

7. Bake for 20-25 minutes, or until the cheese is melted and bubbly.

8. Meanwhile, cook the spaghetti according to package instructions. Drain and serve with the eggplant Parmesan. Garnish with fresh basil.

Thai Green Curry Noodles

Ingredients:

- 8 oz rice noodles
- 1 tbsp olive oil or coconut oil
- 1 onion (chopped)
- 2 cloves garlic (minced)
- 1-inch piece of ginger (grated)
- 1-2 tbsp green curry paste (adjust for spice level)
- 1 can (14 oz) coconut milk
- 1/2 cup vegetable broth
- 1 tbsp soy sauce
- 1 tbsp lime juice
- 1/2 cup bell peppers (sliced)
- 1/2 cup carrots (julienned)
- 1/2 cup snap peas
- Fresh cilantro (for garnish)
- Lime wedges (for serving)

Instructions:

1. Cook the rice noodles according to package instructions. Drain and set aside.

2. In a large pan, heat the oil over medium heat. Add the onion, garlic, and ginger, and sauté for 2-3 minutes until fragrant.

3. Stir in the green curry paste and cook for another minute.

4. Add the coconut milk, vegetable broth, soy sauce, and lime juice. Stir to combine.

5. Add the bell peppers, carrots, and snap peas. Simmer for 5-7 minutes, until the vegetables are tender but still crisp.

6. Toss the cooked rice noodles into the curry sauce and mix to combine.

7. Serve the curry noodles with fresh cilantro and lime wedges on the side.